RICHARD EAST

VANCAT

Meow

ABC
BOOKS

To all those who have known the love of a cat.

I look out over the Australian savanna. The scraggly eucalypts and boab trees are a reminder of just how far I am from my home in Tasmania. Today, I've travelled 300 kilometres on rough outback roads. Just me. And a little black adventure cat named Willow.

No time limits. No worries.

Often, we're far from anything, but everything we need is with us. Our campervan home. Dinner cooking on the camp stove. And each other.

The potholes and corrugations that tested the van all day will be waiting for us tomorrow. But for now, I sit and watch the light change. As the breeze drops, the land feels calm again – and so do I.

Willow circles my legs then jumps up onto my lap. Just like a house cat, she tells me when she needs attention. I scratch her behind the ears. She purrs.

If you'd asked me when I was ten what I'd be doing in twenty years' time, I suspect my answer would have been exactly this. Exploration and adventure – the kinds of things we lose sight of as we're thrown into adulthood. But now, I feel like I have those things back, even though, two years ago, they seemed like an absurd and impossible dream.

The sun is low and paints the sky and everything under it orange. In the stillness, I'm overwhelmed by the feeling that everything's going to be okay.

I didn't always feel this way. When we started on this adventure, contentment, happiness or whatever you want to call it was a difficult feeling to trust. Especially as it felt so foreign ...

B efore I had my van, before I had this life, I had a different van – and a very different life. Back then, I used my van to escape on weekends, when my girlfriend, Gabrielle, and I would venture out into the wilderness of Tasmania.

Our van adventures together took me back to when I was a kid and we went on family camping holidays on Tasmania's east coast. Back in those carefree days we'd swim in the clear cool water and run wild through the bush, following wallaby trails. And while I wouldn't describe myself as particularly adventurous, when I look back, I can see there's always been part of me that needs to be outdoors.

I remember that, when I was about fifteen, I learnt how to windsurf on an old beat-up board. I took it all over the bay, glancing back at the tiny people on the shore. Out in the middle of the bay, near a small island, I'd drop the mast and fall into the ocean. With the sail keeping me afloat, I'd watch the clouds go by. Or, if I was lucky, spot a seal on the reef. Once, I found myself surrounded by fins. A pod of dolphins darted under my board from side to side. They surfaced in the distance then returned, seeming to say, 'Come with us! We'll show you our world!' But I couldn't keep up.

When Gabrielle and I took off in the van for the weekend, I'd forget about the stress of work. I'd stop worrying about the paint peeling off the weatherboards at home and the weeds growing in the backyard. But there was one thing I did worry about, and that was leaving our cats behind.

You see, I'm a cat person. I think I got it from my grandparents. They adored moggies, and the neighbourhood strays knew it, because they'd regularly find their way to my grandparents' doorstep. Each stray was fed and rehabilitated. Most would end up seeing out their days with my grandparents.

My favourite cat of Grandma's was Midas, named after his golden coat. Midas had a bung leg and would sit on the TV cabinet, dangling his leg over the side and obscuring the screen. I still have Grandma's photo album, filled with pictures of all the cats she cared for. On the last page is a photo of me, sitting next to mighty Midas.

Years later, I decided I wanted my own cat. In a shelter, I found a shy little ginger-and-white tomcat named Ty. He was a shorthair, they told me, but two weeks after I'd taken him home, he puffed up into a magnificent cloud of fluff. It turns out he'd had a trim just before I adopted him.

Once, I spent the morning doing a bit of house painting. I took a break for lunch and went inside. In walked Ty, his snout covered in blue dots. I tried to wipe off the paint, but it just spread further. It was perhaps the first and last time anyone has googled 'Can I use mineral turpentine on my cat?'

Ty sported a glorious azure moustache for weeks.

After Gabrielle and I got together, we decided to rescue another cat. This one was black, with a tiny patch of white on her chest and a spark in her character. Gabrielle named her Willow.

Ty seemed to be excited to have a little sister but, less enthused, Willow hissed at him. The standoff continued until Willow established who ruled the house. Soon, however, they were sitting together in front of the fire, washing each other.

Willow is a cat who wants to know what's going on, and she walks with her tail curled like a question mark. So when the doorbell rang, she'd run out to see who was there. She also has good manners. When I put her food down at mealtimes, she'd look up at me and wait for a pat before she started eating. Willow is affectionate, too: at night, she'd sit on our laps for nose boops and cuddles.

As any animal lover will tell you, pets are more than just animals. They share our lives. They comfort us. They're best friends, family, waiting for us to come home each day.

But one day in 2012, Ty didn't come home. Both Ty and Willow were outdoor cats, but they always came home at night. Days later, however, Ty was still missing. Then Dad called. He'd found Ty up the street, dead in the gutter. If only Ty had been as street-smart as he was fluffy, things might have been different.

We buried him next to the fish pond.

It's important to grieve. The gap that pets leave behind is tremendous. For me, grieving for Ty brought back memories of when I was a child and we lost a family cat. It also helped me realise that something else wasn't right. Something the weekend trips in the van would cure for a day or two, before the pain in my chest returned.

I use the phrase 'pain in my chest' because it's so much easier to say than 'chronic anxiety'. It certainly rolls off the tongue better than 'crippling depression'.

But, apart from losing Ty, what did I have to be sad about?

What did I have to worry about?

After all, on the surface, I had it all. I had my own home, job security, friends, a girlfriend. I'd never experienced poverty; I was clothed and fed.

Educated. Employed. Freshly mortgaged. Barbecue and clothesline in the backyard. White picket fence in the front. By all accounts, I had achieved 'The Australian Dream'. And I wasn't even thirty. But I realised that all I felt was an endless spiral of guilt and shame for not appreciating it.

This feeling of dissatisfaction hung over me like a dark cloud. Like heartache without a heartbreak. Some nights, I'd try to lie still enough for my heart to stop racing, still enough that I might sink into the floorboards.

'You can be anything you want, as long as you're happy,' Mum told me.

Shit. I'd even messed that up!

'In ancient times, cats
were worshipped as gods;
they have not forgotten this.'

TERRY PRATCHETT

Things didn't feel so broken when Gabrielle and I went exploring in the van. We didn't leave much of Tasmania uncovered. Little towns. Ancient forests. Rugged coastlines. Empty beaches. On summer afternoons, we'd open all the doors for the breeze. When it was stormy, we'd shelter inside. It was the best of the outdoors with the comfort of indoors.

A happy place on wheels.

But when our weekend escapes ended and we returned home, the impending working week threatened.

Because, in my job in IT, things were deteriorating.

I was underperforming, and I knew it. The guilt of letting my team down was getting to me, but I never opened up about my problems for fear of the consequences. Looking back, I'm sure my employer would have been more than understanding. I persevered alone, but the daily stress, endless projects and overtime were killing me. I was taking days off at a time with tension headaches. And I was running out of excuses. I envied the mind of a cat – unable to experience existential dread.

My motivation hit an all-time low. I struggled to sleep. It was impossible to switch off. At any minute of the day or night, I could be called in to work. I dodged promotion, but the culture there was, if you're not moving up, you're blocking someone else. So I feigned interest in career progression while being determined to stay put. I admire anyone who can thrive in that environment. I could not.

Too scared to actually leave, I daydreamed about quitting. Of winning the lottery and escaping to a desert island. Or maybe to a five-star treehouse in the forest.

It dawned on me that I was enslaved to my mortgage. If I sucked it up for another twenty years, maybe I could retire. That was a bleak thought. Who sold us The Australian Dream, anyway? It was a sham, a scam.

I needed to get away. At least we had our weekend escapes, when Gabrielle and I would head off in the van. One weekend, we ventured past the apple orchards of the Huon Valley into the southern forests. Endless logging roads carved their way across streams and past hidden campsites – perfect for spending a precious night looking up through the trees to the stars.

As we descended a hill beside a recently harvested logging coupe – a scene of pure destruction – the van stalled. No explosion. No bang. Just an eerie silence as we coasted to a stop.

We were 40 kilometres from town, with no phone reception. I knew we were in trouble.

I got out of the van, popped the bonnet and stared into space, lost in thought. If existential dread were a cake, this could be the icing.

I gritted my teeth. Five long minutes passed.

Then, across the valley, I heard the rumble of an engine. A log truck was making its way down the hill. We waved down our guardian angel in flannelette. We were lucky he was working on a Saturday.

Thanks to his kindness, we made it back to civilisation and called a tow truck. I spent a small fortune on repairs then ended up selling the van. Our weekend escapes came to an abrupt end.

What was I doing with my life?

I thought I'd ticked all the boxes. I had a girlfriend. I had a house filled with furniture. A career. But I was empty inside, trudging through life in the direction I thought I ought to be going. I was just playing house.

Now, when I walked into the garden, all I could see were the weeds. The house looked like it was falling apart. Everything was rotten.

One night in early 2014, Gabrielle asked me what was wrong. I broke down crying. We wanted different things. We both had our own problems, and together the result was cataclysmic.

In that moment, I realised our relationship was like that van. There's a point where pouring your heart into something is no use. It was time to walk away.

'A black cat crossing your path signifies that the animal is going somewhere.'

GROUCHO MARX

Gabrielle came by to pick up the last of her stuff. We stood in the kitchen, Willow sprawled on the floor between us.

'I'm not sure if I can take care of Willow. Can you look after her?' Gabrielle asked.

At that point, having not even the remotest idea of what my future would hold, I said yes.

There I was.

Career on the rocks.

Recently single.

Alone in a family suburban home on a quarter acre – close to services with mountain views. I felt homesick in my own house.

I wanted to strip away everything that didn't make me happy and discover who I really was. Throw away all the furniture. The clothes. The garden that no longer brought me joy.

I wanted to tear my whole life to shreds and throw away the rubbish until all that was left were love and optimism.

I wanted to stand under the night sky and scream to the stars, 'Who am I?'

Somebody else could have my job. Somebody else could have this house. Somebody else could have all my things.

I was pacing from room to room, thinking about the events of the past months. Meanwhile, Willow was curled up under a blanket on the couch. Her eyes followed me across the hallway, every time I passed by.

At that moment, I made a choice. I was going to get some help. I owed it to my friends and family to be well. But most of all, I owed it to myself. And to Willow.

I visited my GP, who referred me to a professional. The doctors told me that I was experiencing a minor existential crisis. They reassured me that, as distressing as it may be, my pain was not unlike the pain felt by a guy whose football team has just lost a grand final. That put things into perspective.

Therapy was, for me, a way of learning the language of contentment. A way of changing how my inner voice phrased questions. It was a challenge. But, soon enough, the voice that had fought against me for so many years was on my side. That voice, that inner dialogue, became a source of rationality. It was ready to calmly talk me through my problems. To reassure me when things weren't going well. To see things in perspective.

Eventually, my feelings of self-doubt faded away. Depression was replaced with optimism. Anxiety was replaced with a healthy anticipation for the future. For the first time, I felt like I could truly connect with those around me. Gone were those days of emotional isolation.

As my mental well-being improved, I expected my motivation to return. I was ready to get my career back on track, to really apply myself. In a few years, I thought, maybe I'll take long-service leave and travel the world.

But the exact opposite happened. I completely lost interest in my job. For the first time, I felt I wasn't stuck anymore.

I now had nearly all the pieces to the puzzle.

I just had to fit them together.

The final piece came to me when I was reading an article. It explained that, when we're faced with a choice, our subconscious mind makes the decision well before our conscious mind. Clearly, we give our consciousness far too much credit for how we live our lives. And with it, we waste our energy worrying and overanalysing.

So I threw logic out the window and let intuition take over. I decided to follow my heart.

What my heart wanted was to sell everything I owned, squeeze the few things that made me happy into a campervan and travel Australia indefinitely. I didn't want travel to be an escape from reality. I wanted travel to be my reality.

Okay, fair enough, I thought. Great dream, right there. But how can you afford that? I would have to find a way.

Vans don't run on dreams alone.

I opened up my budget and got to work.

This dream wasn't just a holiday to plan for – it was a whole new way of life. A release from the expenses of urban life. No council rates. No electricity bills. No mortgage repayments or rent. No home maintenance. I added fuel, mobile internet, van servicing and insurance. Laundry. Clothing, food and entertainment would be restricted.

I won't need luxury, I thought. I'll be living a dream bigger than luxury.

I worked out how much it would cost to set up a campervan and how much return I could get from investing the equity in the house after selling.

I added it all up.

It didn't look good.

I paused for a moment, realising I would still have to work. With some adjustments to the numbers, I figured that, if I worked for three months of the year earning minimum wage, I could then travel the rest of the time. It couldn't be simpler. I can do this, I thought. I can make this dream happen.

I didn't have to wait twenty years to start living my life.

It felt strange, making a massive and almost absurd life-changing decision like this without putting much 'conscious' thought into it. But I just let it happen, and it felt good.

I put my house on the market and sorted through my stuff.

The decision to part with something was surprisingly easy. If it was functional in my new life, or increased my happiness, it stayed. Otherwise, it was sold, donated or discarded. My guitar, woodworking tools and board games were in, for example; trinkets, Year Five athletics participation certificates and kitchen gizmos were out. I limited myself to one wooden writing box of keepsakes. I had to be ruthlessly objective in applying this technique. If I hesitated on anything, I photographed then discarded it.

As a trial run, I set aside some containers, equivalent to how much storage a campervan would have, and started living out of those. There were two boxes for kitchen items and food. A small box for toiletries. Two boxes for clothes. Boxes for tools.

As I slowly got rid of everything, it was amazing to see how few things I actually needed or cared for. I was never a hoarder, but the amount of junk I had accumulated in my life was mind-boggling.

An offer came in on the house. I accepted. Now I had a real deadline to work towards. It was time to take the biggest step yet – to leave my job. Despite my struggles, my job still gave me a sense of security. I felt like I was throwing an awful lot away: to say goodbye to that steady income, to my colleagues, to familiarity.

I stopped myself from dwelling on what I was leaving behind and instead focused on what I was taking with me: ten years of experience and life lessons I could apply to any aspect of my life.

I resigned in November 2014. As I made my way back to my office, I felt the most intense feeling of euphoria. I knew I was doing the right thing.

There was one last pressing issue. If I was going to travel off into the sunset in a campervan, I had to contend with a little black cat named Willow. I had no idea who would look after her while I was gone. I had no idea how long I would be gone. I couldn't just take her back to the shelter like returning a library book.

The choice was obvious, my heart told me. Every day, she was there for me. Every night, she fell asleep by my side. I owed it to her to do the best by her.

I decided to take Willow with me.

Within a single week, I had settlement on the house, finished my last day at work and bought my new van.

I got straight to work, converting the van into a tiny house on wheels. This was going to be more than a weekend-escape vehicle. This was a long-term exercise in alternative living. I was embarking on a new way of life and, if I were to make this leap successful, it would have to be a functional space.

I built a kitchen, complete with stove, sink and fridge. Then I made cupboards, drawers, curtains and a bed. Solar panels on the roof and a generator charged a battery bank to power the lights, fridge, laptop and stereo. I installed insulation to keep the inside warm in the cold and tolerable in the northern sun, along with a vent and cabin fan to help keep us cool.

While I was working on the van, Willow would hang out with me. She would explore the new hiding places I was making as our creation came to be.

It took me about a month to get the van to the stage where we could sleep in it. By then, Willow had become familiar with it and would ask to be let in if I had the side door closed. This was promising.

On weekends, Willow and I would drive up the coast to make sure everything I'd worked on that week was in order. The first time, I was hesitant to let her out. I knew she understood that the van was now our home, but I didn't know what would happen if I let her out in a new environment. To my surprise and relief, she handled it just fine.

Seeing her wide-eyed wonder at the new places we visited was heart-warming. Although she never strayed far, I always kept an eye on her to ensure she was safe. She soon learnt that she could climb up the rear ladder onto the roof, and she often spent her time sleeping under the solar panel. When she was ready to come down, her paws made a blood-curdling screech as she slid down the windscreen.

Finally, the van was complete. The best part was being able to sit back and say, 'I built this!'

If you think that I had a plan, you're mistaken. But I had everything I needed. Food. Shelter. And a little black adventure cat with a whole lot of curiosity.

It no longer mattered where I was heading. To the old me, this would have been frightening.

Now, if I found myself dwelling on it, I would remember something the philosopher Alan Watts once said. That life is not a journey or a pilgrimage. Instead, it's like a work of art, such as a dance or a beautiful piece of music. We always push ourselves to that next step in life, knowing that around the corner there may be success, or the realisation of our dreams, but we forget one thing. To live for today.

It was something Willow knew all along. And she was showing me how to do it.

There she was, by my side, as I made the biggest changes of my life. It was such a comfort to know I had her with me.

What better way to live for today than by spending it with your best friend? This rescue cat had now rescued me.

In May 2015, after saying goodbye to our family and friends, Willow and I boarded the ferry in Devonport that would take us from our island home of Tasmania to the even bigger island home of mainland Australia. We had done it. Everything I'd worked towards over the past months had come to fruition.

I watched the port disappear.

What happened next didn't matter.

'Way down deep, we're all motivated by the same urges. Cats have the courage to live by them.'

JIM DAVIS

The nights were cold as we passed through Victoria. On the Murray River, we camped under towering gum trees. We passed houseboats moored on the opposite bank and fishermen angling for the prized Murray cod.

Before we left, I'd bought a radio-frequency tracker that attached to Willow's collar. The tracker would tell me in which direction she was and how far. Then at each place, I had to make a choice: keep her on a leash or set her free to explore. It all depended on whether it was safe for Willow and for the environment. The decision to let her free was never one I took lightly. But, just like humans, Willow wanted to be free to wander and play. To discover and explore. So, sometimes, I'd take a risk.

One afternoon, about a month into our adventure, I let Willow out to explore.

I kept an eye on her as I cooked dinner.

But then she was gone.

I'd lost my cat.

I turned on Willow's radio-frequency tracker but couldn't get a signal. So I walked through the campsite and into the night.

Still, I couldn't pick up a signal. The temperature dropped to freezing. Finally, at two o'clock in the morning, I gave up and went to bed. Perhaps I'd wake to the familiar sound of her sliding down the windscreen.

I woke up feeling sick.

Who takes their cat camping? Let alone around Australia? I berated myself.

I'd been a fool.

Rugging up, I set out again. This time, I systematically expanded my search, and eventually crossed the highway. I must have walked 15 kilometres that day before darkness descended on another freezing night. As I walked down yet another track, moonlight reflected in the puddles.

Then I heard a beep. And another. The tracker lit up in my hand. I hurtled through the bush, waving spider webs out of my face. My imagination took over: what if she's been eaten by a river yowie and I'm being lured into its lair?!

Then the beeps stopped.

Perhaps I'd scared her away. Either way, I'd lost the signal and any hope of holding her in my arms that night.

I returned to the van. Inside, it was 4 degrees Celsius. I left the door open again all night, but no Willow.

The next morning, I made a plan. I'd figured that Willow must have crossed the road when it was quiet but became too scared to cross back when the traffic picked up. So I moved the van close to where I last received a signal from her collar. But I was running out of batteries for the tracker – it was my last chance.

Of course, a cat is not easily persuaded, nor can a cat be placed, set or positioned. Only a fool would attempt to change the will of a cat.

In fact, there's no such thing as a lost cat, only a cat whose notion of where it should be differs from your own. Such is the will of a cat.

Still, I figured that Willow would most likely sleep all day. So, that evening, I headed back out again, stepping quietly with tracker in hand, before sitting down to wait, shivering in my coat.

I heard a beep. Then another! I kept calm and stopped myself from running to her.

'Willow, Willow,' I called softly.

The lights on the tracker turned from red to orange. She was coming closer.

'Willow.'

The lights were now green. I shone the torch down the track and saw two eyes reflected back at me. I was shaking, but Willow just strolled calmly towards me before sitting down and wrapping her tail around my leg.

I picked up my cat with tears in my eyes, holding her so tight.

I realised one thing that day. Willow and I have a bond. An unspoken agreement. She will always come back to me, and I will never leave her behind.

We moved quickly those first few months, compared to these days, anyway. From the Murray River, we drove up to Canberra and east to Bateman's Bay. Then up the coast to Sydney then Brisbane.

On the long highways, I often saved money by offering a lift to backpackers. They'd chip in fuel money and, more importantly, keep me awake.

After a 1700-kilometre haul up the Bruce Highway, we arrived in Cairns.

After saying goodbye to a backpacker with whom we'd just exchanged life stories, we headed to the docks. I wanted to see the Great Barrier Reef.

The SV *Watermusic* was a 48-foot sailing boat. It was a floating community of travellers. Rob, the owner, had to make three trips in his bright orange dinghy to ferry everyone onboard.

Plus a little cat.

Boat cats are not a new concept. Sailors used to choose Maine Coons as mousers, as their big paws could grip the deck in storms. But as we set sail, I wondered how Willow would fare. Fortunately, the fair weather meant she soon found her sea paws.

We moored at Fitzroy Island, roughly 30 kilometres south-east of Cairns. While the humans snorkelled with the turtles, Willow searched the cabin for the perfect quiet napping spot.

When we returned to the boat, I used Willow's tracker to find which cupboard she was sleeping in. Then, while everyone helped out to make dinner, she found the most obtrusive spot on the cabin floor to spread out.

We watched the last of the sun from the deck before bed.

The sticky sea air was still when we woke. The hum of the tourist boats approaching reminded us that we would soon have to share paradise.

By evening, the other tourists had left and, for one last night, we had the reef to ourselves again.

As I travelled up and down Australia's east coast in 2015, I met people who had escaped the city for a simpler life – to live off the land and be free. They seemed to have figured out what they truly need in life then put that plan into action. They'd said goodbye to the coffees and brunches. To the new cars, expensive clothes and other symbols of status.

And I was finding that it's not a big sacrifice when you're rewarded with time to spend with those you care most about. It's not about shirking consumerism – not entirely. It's about taking only what we need.

Why sacrifice our freedom for someone else's greed?

A good way to save money on the road is to volunteer. There are many schemes that bring together travellers and farms, families and projects that need help. Often, the hosts will feed and house their guests in exchange for a few hours' work each day.

I met a couple in the Glasshouse Mountains, Queensland, and ended up staying a week to dig their garden. Willow enjoyed the extra attention and her time exploring the garden. It felt good to help others achieve their dream. In return, I was rewarded with delicious home-cooked meals and stories.

We left well-fed and content.

'Time spent with cats
is never wasted.'

SIGMUND FREUD

Willow isn't much of a hiking cat. So, while I describe her as an adventure cat, the truth is she's predominantly a napping cat.

We were returning south to New South Wales before the warmer months arrived. One evening, we parked at Brunswick Heads in northern New South Wales. We were making our way along a track behind the dunes, Willow walking some distance ahead of me. As I shone the torch in her direction, I was startled by the presence of a 2-metre diamond python. How Willow had passed the snake without noticing, I have no idea. But there we were. I was on one side. Then a snake. And Willow on the other. Do pythons eat cats? I wondered.

Willow stared at me.

Olive-coloured, with darker, diamond-shaped markings covering its length, the python was a beautiful creature.

Even though diamond pythons are non-venomous, I decided to give this one a wide circle. I cut through the scrub to the other side then grabbed my cat. After we made it the long way back down the track, I thought it best to call it a night.

In April 2016, we ventured north again through central Queensland. Summer was over, so I figured it would now be cool enough for our Tassie blood. Not that I didn't have the air-conditioning covered. My system was simple. We drove north in winter, south in summer.

In any case, a van is adaptable. If it's hot, you park in the shade. If it's cold, you point the windscreen north. If you don't like your neighbours, you move on.

I'd insulated the van to help endure the outback sun, so it was tolerable. Most importantly, Willow was comfortable. I could always board her in a cattery or at a vet if the weather was too extreme, but fortunately, it never came to that.

We'd travelled the coast road on our first foray up north. So this time we travelled the inland roads. Coming through Emerald and Longreach in May 2016, it dawned on me just how far we were from home. Savanna extended to the horizon. Highways stretched for days. It was so unlike the forested valleys and winding roads I'd grown up with.

Finding places to stay in outback Queensland involved a mixture of camp guidebooks, satellite imagery and pure determination. Many times, we would arrive to find the campsite unsuitable for a cat.

No pets allowed.

Too close to the road.

There would be no choice but to drive on.

When we did find a place to call home for the night, Willow would jump out, keen to explore the camp and suss out her next napping spot. She'd make herself at home in an instant.

I'd watch her play as I cooked dinner. Then I'd put out two chairs – she always took the good one.

After visiting Mount Isa, in north-west Queensland, I made a snap decision to go further north to Burketown. It was the end of May and the start of the dry season. About 300 kilometres of gravel road lay between us and our destination.

The road was full of ruts from the last wet season. Untold bumps and jolts later, we pulled into the township of Burketown. Still 20 kilometres of crocodile-infested mangroves lay between us and the Gulf of Carpentaria.

At that moment, I realised I wanted to see the Gulf – even though the thought had never previously crossed my mind. It was certainly never on my 'bucket list'. Probably because I don't believe in them. For me, bucket lists are a morbid thought. After all, what do you do when you have ticked everything off? Just keel over? What if you don't get to tick everything off? Is that a life unlived?

I asked a local about the road conditions.

She paused, thinking. The road west through to Borroloola was passable, certainly, she said, but it was mostly unsealed with some difficult sections at the end. The phrase she used was 'rough and ready'.

I've come to learn something about roads. The further a road is from the person you ask, the more dangerous they say it is. It must be our fear of the unfamiliar.

So, thinking that the road couldn't possibly be too bad, we headed west.

As it turned out, it wasn't the roughest road we'd been on, but it was, by far, the most unrelenting. Corrugations shook the van. Dry creek crossings meant sudden dips in the road, and sometimes they were far from dry.

The potholes were both abundant and deceptive.

At first, the 110 kilometres per hour speed limit seemed crazy, but it wasn't so bad once you got used to it.

There was not even a peep out of Willow during the entire trip. And at the end of the day, she still looked like a princess. I, meanwhile, was covered in dust.

About one third of the way along the road to Borroloola lay Hell's Gate Roadhouse. It proved to be a fitting name for the place. The sides of the road on approach were littered with car bodies. Outside the roadhouse was a burnt-out semi, its tyres shredded. Apparently, a week earlier, the truck was ten minutes from the settlement when the brakes jammed and caught fire. Panicking, the driver dumped the trailer to lighten the load and motored on to the roadhouse to avoid being stranded in the outback. Somehow in the process, he broke both his ankles. It would have been a sight to see, the truck screeching in, all aflame.

These were rough roads. Before this adventure, I'd never even changed a tyre. In the first year that Willow and I were on the road, we blew four tyres. Not that Willow was ever inconvenienced. She'd just keep napping in the back of the van.

Hundreds of kilometres of corrugations later, we reached Borroloola then headed north. Eventually, in the first week of June, we arrived at the Bing Bong Port Facility, which turned out to be just a loading facility and a few houses. I got out of the van and gazed at the vast expanse of blue sea and sky. We'd reached the Gulf.

Climbing back into the van, we continued on our way.

Three days later, we crossed into Western Australia and headed in the direction of Port Hedland, on the north coast of that state. We were now deep in the Pilbara region, where the land is so flat, it's almost claustrophobic.

In mid-July, we camped at Split Rock, east of Port Hedland and not far off the highway. It looked like a safe place to pull in for a night or three.

There are three monoliths at Split Rock, and as soon as I let Willow out, she started to climb one. I followed closely behind. Willow glided effortlessly over the loose rocks while I stumbled. It was heart-warming to see: no leash, no harness. Just doing what a cat does best.

At the top, we watched the sun sink below the horizon. Feeling like we were high above the earth, we gazed across the Australian savanna.

Road trains passed in the distance. So did the day's worries. Not that there were many.

A day's drive beyond Port Hedland lay the town of Exmouth. We took a week to get there. Our visit to Exmouth was significant. We'd now been on the road for a year and three months, and had reached the farthest geographical distance from our home town of Hobart, as the crow flies.

I wasn't sure how to celebrate this milestone. Was it worthy of celebration at all?

We parked on the headland. As Willow continued her morning nap, I took a walk along the dunes. Then I heard someone shout.

I looked around. The beach was empty.

The voice called again. 'Do you want a beer?'

I looked out over the sand. Still no one.

'DO YOU WANT A BEER?!'

I realised the voice was coming from a dinghy, 30 metres off the beach.

Now, I've come to know that refusing generosity is to deny someone the joy of kindness. This was no exception.

'Yes!' I shouted. 'Yes, I would like a beer!'

The two people in the dinghy motored towards the beach. I waded out and jumped in, my shorts soaked. Sitting in the middle of the boat was a full esky. We shared a few beers and a few stories, then they dropped me back on the beach. I watched them motor away.

'Cats are connoisseurs of comfort.'

JAMES HERRIOT

Finding places to camp in Western Australia was tricky. Pastoral leases make up one third of the state and border onto highways, so there's very little free land to explore. The southern forests are also a problem for pet owners, due to feral-baiting programs. Poisoning by 1080 is a horrible way for an animal to die.

Many cattle stations do allow travellers onto their leasehold for a fee. In fact, some have established campgrounds and caravan parks. So after leaving Exmouth, we visited Gnaraloo Station, near the southern end of Ningaloo Reef. It's a stunning place – red earth on one side, coral reef on the other and some pretty serious surf breaks, too. No wonder thousands visit it every year.

Willow and I stayed for a couple of days, but then we needed to move on. I just don't like crowds. Call me selfish, but I like my own space. Willow agrees. I prefer the stillness, away from the traffic. Away from everything. But I rarely get lonely. You're never alone with a cat.

Sometimes, though, solitude has its limit.

We reached the city of Perth in September. There we stayed with friends, right in the city. We'd intended to stay for a week, but that week turned into the whole summer. My friends got me a job in a bar, and Willow became a city cat. It's always surprising how well she adapts.

Even though we were in the city, Willow and I still slept in the van. But no matter whether we were staying in a house or the van, Willow always knew where to find me for her dinner.

City life felt extravagant. Meals out, running hot water – I felt spoilt. I was earning money, too, but I was spending it just as fast. It was an amazing summer but, in January 2017, I was keen to get on the road again.

We planned to head east from Perth via Esperance. But in early February, Western Australia was hit by some of the worst floods the state had suffered in years. We arrived in Jerramungup, on the southern coast of Western Australia, to discover that the road east to Ravensthorpe was closed. The Phillips River Bridge had been washed away, leaving Ravensthorpe completely stranded.

We waited for three days but, with no sign of the floodwaters receding and alternative routes created, I decided to backtrack and take a 1200-kilometre detour north to Kalgoorlie.

When you don't really know where you're going, a change of plans isn't such a big deal.

In the last days of February 2017, we crossed the Nullarbor into South Australia. Willow had finally visited every state and territory in Australia. I congratulated her on her 'Purrfect Eight'.

When we started out, I had counted the days since we'd left home. Days became months. Then years.

Do I count the places we've been?

Do I count the distance we've travelled together?

These numbers don't mean anything, really.

People would often ask me where we were travelling to, and I stumbled for an answer. In the early days, I often woke up wondering where we should be. Now, I realised we were already there. The sense of urgency to move on had passed. We'd settled into this life. It didn't matter where we were.

'Travellers' was no longer the right term for us. We were 'nomads'.

If someone were to publish a book called *The Ultimate Australian Road Trip for Cats*, one of the destinations would be the Matthew Flinders statue in Port Lincoln, South Australia, which features the great navigator and cartographer with Trim, his faithful cat. Trim was born a boat cat and joined Flinders on his circumnavigation of Australia from 1801 to 1803. Trim even survived a shipwreck.

We made it to Port Lincoln in March 2017. Visiting the statue to pay our respects to the first cat that circumnavigated Australia was a proud moment.

Willow's travels aren't unique, after all.

We've encountered many travelling cats along our way, many people doing exactly what we are doing. Then there are those unfamiliar with the concept.

Once a backpacker came up to me and said, 'Excuse me! There's a black cat trying to get into your van!'

'I know.'

Others ask me why she doesn't run away. This seems like a strange question. Why would she run away from me? I'm an okay guy!

A scared cat will run and hide. When they feel safe, they'll return to you. If you chase after them, they'll keep running. Willow knows her safe place is with me and the van. She always returns. I understand that I take a risk letting her out, but I feel it's a justifiable one.

The southern mangroves near Port Germein, South Australia, are a beautiful place to explore – and free of crocs. There you can watch the tide turn, the water rising over the spreading roots of the mangrove trees. When the tide goes out, you can walk out for up to a kilometre. From out there I could see my van, a tiny white spot in the distance. Into that tiny house on wheels was packed my whole life.

But the mangroves also seem to be the location of many of our misadventures. One night, when we were camped there, I let Willow out for a walk. I was just a moment behind her, and a half-moon cast enough light to see the spreading veins of the creek.

Then I lost sight of my cat.

I walked further in, but there was still no sign. I shone my torch through the swamp. Then I heard a distressed meow. Where had she got to? I turned on her tracker.

At last I spotted her, on the other side of a small creek and dense mangroves. I had no idea how she'd made it through. She meowed louder, and my 'caternal' instincts kicked in. I made a dash through the creek, my feet sinking further into the mud with every step, the mangrove branches scraping my back. When I finally reached Willow, she looked at me as if nothing was wrong.

Together we took the long way back. Willow, clean and dry, followed closely behind me, soaked and covered in mud.

On another occasion, a few months later, we'd parked up in the mangroves near Port Pirie, close to town so we could get to the farmers' market in the morning. It was a place we'd camped at many times before. After dinner, we decided to go for a walk. I opened the sliding door, but Willow refused to jump out. When I shone the torch, I realised we were parked in water.

Like an idiot, I'd forgotten to check the tides.

Again.

A week earlier, I'd made a similar mistake. Willow had jumped out, and I heard a splash. At first, I was confused. She looked up at me, the tide lapping at her belly. Then she ran (or swam) around the side of the van. I climbed out, grabbed her and wrapped her in a towel before she could jump on our clean bed.

This time, it was worse – the road now looked like it was under a foot of water. We were parked on a rise, so my options were limited: stay there overnight and wait for the water to recede, or make a dash for it.

I decided to get out of there.

I slowly edged the van onto the road. There were 400 metres of foot-deep water between us and safety, with a deep creek on one side. Instantly regretting my decision, I tried to reverse back. The wheels spun. Okay, so the only way was forwards.

I climbed out and kicked the mud from underneath the tyres. With wet feet, I put the van into low gear and continued along the road. The van pushed through the water, fishtailing all the way. As the wheels found the ruts in the road, we were carried along like a log on a theme-park flume ride.

Eventually, we made it to higher ground and a drier campsite.

'Lucky you wanted to stay dry, you clever cat,' I said to Willow, relieved. 'Those sausage rolls and cream cakes at the farmers' market will be ours tomorrow after all.'

I've learnt that the weather can change quickly. Storms can come in fast and roads can flood. And when your only shelter is a van, you're exposed to it all.

And I've learnt to never underestimate the tides.

Happiness can be fleeting. As soon as you feel that you have a hold of it, you open your hand and it's gone. Living costs and rent prices are rising. It's becoming harder to buy your own home, to find happiness in the life of consumerism we've all been sold.

It's no wonder that many of those struggling to make do are tuning out in favour of a better life on the road. A life on their terms. Others are simply searching for well-being and a richer experience.

During our travels, Willow and I have met a whole community of people on similar paths to ours. People who have made the transition to a simpler life. Many are on a path to find themselves. Some are searching for something they once lost. Others are looking for meaning.

I haven't found a reason, and I don't think I will.

I'll just settle for absurdism – the conflict between our desire to seek the meaning of life and our inability to find it.

But when I look back on my life before we left Tasmania, I realise that what I thought was a mid-life crisis was actually a mid-life opportunity.

An opportunity to let go of everything holding me back. To wake up every morning and appreciate what I have. It's been a lesson in gratitude, and I owe thanks to a little black adventure cat named Willow, who helped me learn that lesson.

Not that you have to be adventurous to travel. In fact, I wonder whether Willow and I have redefined the term 'adventure'. For Willow, it's all about napping in new and unusual places, and I fully support her in this endeavour. We don't have to climb Everest. We can simply go somewhere we've never been before.

Ten days is a comfortable amount of time to stay in one spot. By then, rations will be low and so will clean clothes. Once all the fresh produce and meat goes, the cooking gets creative. I make my own flat breads, yoghurt, sprouts and pickles.

A local angler may be kind enough to give us some fish from their haul, sensing, perhaps, that I don't know one end of a fishing rod from the other. Of course, Willow also gets a snack – a tiny piece of cheese or a scrap of meat. Nothing brings me more joy than the sound of a cat eating a potato chip. In moderation, of course.

We'll go into town together to stock up on supplies and fuel. Visit the laundromat. Willow will sleep in the van the whole time, except to inspect the groceries. Sometimes, we'll move on. Other times, we'll return to the same place. There are places we can't go, such as national parks and conservation areas. But I never feel we miss out. We've seen parts of Australia I never knew existed.

We've camped by lakes and mountains. Forests and deserts. Next to power stations and abandoned buildings. On beaches that would rival a five-star resort.

I used to feel cynical about life, lonely in crowds, disconnected. Now I feel a part of the world. When someone walks by, I wave. I might start chatting, and there's a good chance we'll spend some time sharing our lives.

Sometimes, you have to trust yourself and follow your intuition.

Sometimes, you have to do something a little crazy.

What I thought I needed to make me happy differed greatly from what I really needed. For me, The Australian Dream isn't dead, it just needed some wheels.

'I have studied many philosophers and many cats. The wisdom of cats is infinitely superior.'

HIPPOLYTE TAINE

In November 2017, Willow and I passed from South Australia to Victoria and travelled along the Great Ocean Road. When we arrived in Melbourne, our lap of Australia was complete. It had taken us 900 days – almost three years. We boarded the ferry to Tasmania and headed straight to the east coast.

Together we camped on a beach we'd visited together three years before. I took a photo of Willow on the granite boulders overlooking the water. I'd spent my summers growing up here, playing in this same turquoise water. Home may be wherever we park our van, but some places feel more like home than others. This was one of those.

The story doesn't end here. Willow and I are still travelling. Although one stage of our adventure has ended, there's more to come. This is our life now. I can't imagine what my travels would have been like without Willow. Somehow, I don't think I would have made it this far.

Acknowledgements

Mum and Dad, for only ever being a phone call away, and for posting chocolate biscuits to me in the outback.

Steph, for your love, even when there's an ocean between us.

Jai, my friend, mentor and hero.

Katie, for convincing me that an idea could become a book.

Jude, Barbara and the rest of the HarperCollins team, for turning that idea into a reality.

Willow's friends across the globe, who check in on us daily and send messages of support.

And, of course, Willow – my light, my shadow.

The ABC 'Wave' device is a trademark of
the Australian Broadcasting Corporation
and is used under licence by
HarperCollins*Publishers* Australia.

First published in Australia in 2019
by HarperCollins*Publishers* Australia Pty Limited
ABN 36 009 913 517
harpercollins.com.au

HarperCollins*Publishers*
Level 13, 201 Elizabeth Street, Sydney, NSW 2000, Australia
Unit D1, 63 Apollo Drive, Rosedale, Auckland 0632,
    New Zealand
A 53, Sector 57, Noida, UP, India
1 London Bridge Street, London, SE1 9GF, United Kingdom
Bay Adelaide Centre, East Tower, 22 Adelaide Street West,
    41st Floor, Toronto, Ontario, M5H 4E3, Canada
195 Broadway, New York, NY 10007, USA

A catalogue record for this book is available
from the National Library of Australia

ISBN: 978 0 7333 3956 1 (paperback)

Cover and internal design by HarperCollins Design Studio
Layout and typesetting by Jane Waterhouse
Photography by Richard East
Background textures by shuttterstock.com
Colour reproduction by Graphic Print Group, Adelaide SA
Printed and bound in China by RR Donnelley